28 Lives History Forgot

A Month of Remarkable People Who
Changed the World Quietly

Edwin Hale

Contents

Introduction   v

Part 1
Survival, Courage, and the Cost of Being Seen

1 Ona Judge	3
2 Mayken van Angola	9
3 Elizabeth Jennings	13
4 Nancy Hart	17
5 James Hemings	21
6 Anton Wilhelm Amo	25
7 Thayendanegea (Joseph Brant)	29

Part 2
Building Change from the Inside

8 Lemuel Haynes	35
9 James Forten	39
10 Esther de Berdt Reed	43
11 Hannah Griffitts	47
12 Eliza Harriot O'Connor	51
13 Trota of Salerno	55
14 Jeanne Villepreux-Power	59

Part 3
The Quiet Architecture of Everyday Life

15 Margaret E. Knight	65
16 Josephine Cochrane	69
17 Nancy Johnson	73
18 Anne Connelly	77
19 Maria Beasley	81

20 Eleanor Coade	85
21 Henrietta Vansittart	89

Part 4
Expanding the World

22 Sake Dean Mahomed	95
23 Jeanne Baret	99
24 Lewis Latimer	103
25 Eunice Newton Foote	107
26 Sophie Germain	111
27 Oliver Heaviside	115
28 Jeanne Villepreux-Power	119
What These Lives Ask of Us	123
Sources and Further Reading	127
Acknowledgements	131

Introduction

Why Some Lives Fade and
Why We Need Them Now

History, as it is usually told, prefers clean lines and loud names. It remembers kings more easily than cooks, generals more readily than gardeners, and inventors more often than the hands that refined their ideas.

> *The story of the past becomes narrow not because few people mattered, but because only a few were allowed to be remembered.*

This book begins from a quieter assumption. That the world we live in was shaped not only by those whose names appear in monuments and textbooks, but by countless people whose work was practical, intimate, and often invisible. People who solved problems without applause. People who endured systems that were never designed for them and still left something better behind.

Introduction

Lives fade from history for many reasons. Some people lacked wealth or social standing, some were women, enslaved, colonized, or "just" working-class. Some lived before their ideas had language or acceptance. Others were overshadowed by more powerful figures who absorbed the credit. In many cases, forgetting was not an accident. It was a consequence.

> Yet absence from the record does not mean absence from impact.

The buildings we pass, the tools we use, the food we eat, the freedoms we assume, and even the scientific truths we now take for granted often trace back to individuals whose names we no longer speak. Their influence survives even when their stories do not.

This book is not an attempt to correct history in full. That would be impossible. *It is instead an invitation to pause and look closer.* To spend one month with twenty-eight lives that history moved past too quickly. Each chapter offers a brief encounter rather than a comprehensive biography. A moment, a choice, a contribution, and the quiet echo that followed.

February is a short month.

It asks for attention rather than endurance.

> Reading one life a day mirrors the way these people lived.

Introduction

Incrementally. Persistently. Without knowing how, or if, they would be remembered.

These stories are not unified by heroism in the traditional sense. They are connected by something smaller and more human. Resolve. Curiosity. Care. The decision to act within limited circumstances. Some of the people in these pages succeeded. Some failed. Some paid dearly for what they did. All of them altered the world in ways that outlasted them.

> Remembering them now is not an exercise in nostalgia. It is a way of widening our understanding of how change happens.

Progress is rarely a single moment or a single person. It is more often the accumulation of quiet lives doing necessary work.

What follows is not a replacement for the history you already know. It is a companion to it. A reminder that the past was crowded, complicated, and full of people whose stories are still worth telling...

Part 1
Survival, Courage, and the Cost of Being Seen
Day 1-7

1 Ona Judge
The Courage to Stay Gone

Ona Judge knew exactly what would happen if she stayed.

She had grown up inside one of the most powerful households in the new United States, surrounded by polished manners and carefully rehearsed ideals about liberty. She listened as freedom was discussed at the dinner table, as independence was praised in public speeches, as the language of rights spread through the city of Philadelphia. None of it applied to her.

Ona was enslaved by Martha Washington and worked as her personal attendant. Her days were shaped by proximity. She dressed the First Lady, attended her closely, and learned how power moved by watching it at arm's length. This closeness was not protection. It was exposure. She was visible, useful, and entirely owned.

By her early twenties, Ona had learned something that many enslaved people learned too late. She was about to be passed on. Martha Washington planned to give her as a wedding gift to her granddaughter. It would be a permanent transfer. New owners. New expectations. No recourse.

Ona decided she would not wait.

In 1796, while the Washington household prepared for dinner, Ona Judge walked out of the President's house and disappeared into the city. She did not leave with luggage. She did not leave with papers. She left with the certainty that staying meant losing the last scraps of control she had over her own life.

What followed was not a clean escape. It was a long act of resistance.

Philadelphia was dangerous for a fugitive. Slave catchers operated openly, and the Fugitive Slave Act allowed enslavers to pursue people across state lines. George Washington was not an ordinary enslaver. He had resources, influence, and the machinery of the federal government behind him.

He used it.

Washington placed advertisements describing Ona's appearance in detail. He sent agents to track her movements. He pressured officials to quietly return her without public embarrassment. When those efforts failed, he escalated.

Ona had fled north and eventually reached New Hampshire, where she married a free Black man and began a precarious new life. She lived with constant risk. Washington's agents came close to capturing her more than once. Each time, she escaped again. Each time, she chose to stay gone.

This is the part of the story that often gets compressed into a single sentence. "She escaped and lived free." The reality was far harsher.

Freedom, for Ona Judge, did not mean safety or comfort. It meant poverty, illness, and fear. It meant knowing that any unfamiliar knock at the door could end her life as she had rebuilt it. It meant watching her children struggle, sometimes hungry, sometimes sick, while knowing that returning would guarantee food but cost everything else.

Years later, when asked whether she regretted her decision, Ona did not soften her answer.

She said she would rather suffer and be free than live in comfort as a slave.

That sentence is easy to quote. It is harder to sit with.

Ona Judge was not chasing an abstract ideal. She was choosing autonomy over survival as defined by others. She was refusing a system that demanded gratitude for her own captivity. She was asserting that her life belonged to her, even if that life was difficult and short.

What makes her story uncomfortable is not just the hypocrisy it exposes, though that is undeniable. The man celebrated as the father of American liberty never stopped trying to recapture her. He did not question whether he had the right. He questioned only how discreetly it could be done.

What makes the story powerful is Ona's clarity. She did not frame her escape as heroic. She framed it as necessary.

Ona Judge lived the rest of her life outside the official record. She never gained wealth or status. She did not publish her story. It survives because she agreed, late in life, to speak with abolitionist newspapers who recorded her words.

She knew the risk of speaking. She also knew the cost of silence.

In telling her story, Ona reclaimed something slavery was designed to erase. Self-definition. She named herself as the central figure in her own life, not a supporting character in someone else's legacy.

History often measures courage by spectacle. Battles fought. Speeches delivered. Laws signed. Ona Judge's courage was quieter and more sustained. It was the courage to endure consequences without the promise of reward. The courage to wake up every day and choose freedom again.

She did not get to be remembered as a symbol in her own time. She did not get monuments or textbooks. What she left behind instead was a truth that still unsettles. Freedom is not granted by ideals alone. It is claimed, protected, and lived, often at great personal cost.

Ona Judge stayed gone. That was her revolution.

2 Mayken van Angola
Freedom Won One
Signature at a Time

Mayken van Angola did not escape in the night.

She went to court.

In the early seventeenth century, New Amsterdam was a small, rough settlement balanced between commerce and survival. It was governed by the Dutch West India Company, a trading enterprise more concerned with profit than principle. Slavery existed there openly, but it was not yet fixed into the rigid racial system it would later become. That instability created narrow cracks. Mayken found one and pushed.

Little is known about Mayken's early life. Her name suggests she was taken from the region Europeans called Angola, though that word flattened many cultures into a single label. By the time she appears in the records, she was enslaved in New Netherland, performing labor that sustained a colony that denied her personhood.

She was also a mother.

When Mayken's husband died, her situation worsened. Enslaved women were especially vulnerable. Without a male partner, their labor and their bodies were often treated as assets to be reassigned. Their children were considered property. Survival required more than endurance. It required strategy.

Mayken chose the law.

In 1644, she joined a small group of enslaved Africans who petitioned the Dutch authorities for what was called half-freedom. The request was extraordinary. It asked for legal recognition as free people, with the obligation to pay an annual fee and provide labor when demanded. Their children, however, would remain enslaved.

It was a compromise so stark it is difficult to read without anger. Freedom that did not extend to one's own children is not freedom in any full sense. And yet Mayken agreed.

Why would she?

Because half-freedom was still freedom in motion.

The petition was granted. Mayken became one of the first women of African descent in the colony to secure a form of legal liberty. She could live independently. She could work for wages. She could appear in court not as property, but as a person.

And she did.

Mayken van Angola returned to the courts again and again, each time pushing the boundary a little further. She sued for unpaid wages. She defended her property. She demanded the rights promised to her under Dutch law. Every appearance left another mark in the record. Another assertion that she belonged to herself.

Her life was still constrained. She owed annual payments to the company. She remained under threat of re-enslavement if she failed to meet her obligations. Her children were not free. The system was designed to keep her negotiating from a position of weakness.

But negotiation itself was power.

What makes Mayken's story remarkable is not that she won everything. It is that she understood freedom as something that could be assembled piece by piece. A document. A payment. A court appearance. A name written down where it was not supposed to be.

She lived in a world that did not imagine her as a legal actor. She forced it to do so anyway.

Over time, the legal footholds claimed by people like Mayken helped shape a free Black community in what would later become New York. Their petitions and lawsuits created precedents that unsettled the idea that enslavement was natural or permanent. The colony eventually shifted toward harsher racial slavery, but the record of resistance remained.

Mayken van Angola does not appear in grand narratives of abolition. Her name is found instead in dry documents and court proceedings. Ink on paper. Transactions. Signatures. These are not the places we are taught to look for courage.

Yet her life reminds us that freedom is not always seized in a single act. Sometimes it is negotiated under pressure, defended repeatedly, and protected through persistence rather than force.

Mayken did not leave a manifesto. She left a paper trail.

And in doing so, she demonstrated something enduring. Even within systems built to deny humanity, there are moments when insistence reshapes reality. One signature at a time.

3 Elizabeth Jennings

The Carriage Ride That
Changed Public Space

Elizabeth Jennings was running late.

It was a Sunday morning in July 1854, and she was on her way to church in New York City. She was neatly dressed, carrying herself with the quiet confidence of a young woman who knew who she was. Elizabeth was a teacher. She was well educated. She was also Black, and that fact would decide how the rest of her morning unfolded.

When the streetcar arrived, Elizabeth stepped on as any paying passenger would. Almost immediately, the conductor told her to get off. Black riders, he said, were not allowed inside. She refused.

This was not an impulsive decision. Elizabeth knew the rules as they existed. She also knew how arbitrary they were. Segregation on New York's streetcars was unevenly enforced and often justified with vague claims about custom rather than law. Conductors were given discretion, and discretion usually meant exclusion.

The conductor tried to force her off. Elizabeth held her ground.

What followed was not a quiet disagreement. She was dragged from the car. Her bonnet was torn. Her dress was damaged. A policeman was called, not to protect her, but to help remove her. She was thrown onto the street in front of other passengers and left there humiliated and injured.

Elizabeth did not disappear afterward. She did not accept what had happened as inevitable.

Instead, she went home and told her father.

Thomas L. Jennings was not a man accustomed to silence. He was a successful tailor and an abolitionist who believed deeply in the law as a tool, even when it failed. Together, father and daughter decided to sue the streetcar company.

This decision mattered. Lawsuits required money, time, and public exposure. They required faith that the system might listen. Elizabeth was willing to put her name and her experience on record.

The case went to court the following year. Elizabeth testified calmly about what had happened. Witnesses confirmed her account. The defense argued that segregation was standard practice. The judge disagreed.

Elizabeth Jennings won.

The ruling did not instantly desegregate New York's public transit, but it cracked the door open. The court affirmed that Black passengers who behaved properly could not be excluded solely because of race. It gave legal standing to a simple but powerful idea. Public space belonged to the public.

The impact spread. Other lawsuits followed. Pressure built. Within a few years, New York's streetcars were formally desegregated.

Elizabeth returned to her life. She continued teaching. She did not go on a speaking tour. She did not seek attention. History did not rush to celebrate her.

But her carriage ride changed the city.

What makes Elizabeth Jennings's story easy to overlook is how ordinary it begins. She wanted to go to church. She paid her fare. She expected to arrive on time. There was no plan to make history that morning.

That ordinariness is the point.

Public space is where power quietly asserts itself. Who is allowed to sit, to ride, to linger, to belong. Elizabeth understood that exclusion works best when it feels routine. She interrupted that routine by refusing to move.

Her resistance was not loud. It was firm. It was rooted in self-respect rather than spectacle. She did not argue that she was exceptional. She argued that she was entitled.

Nearly a century before Rosa Parks, Elizabeth Jennings demonstrated that civil rights battles often begin not with speeches, but with bodies refusing to be displaced. With someone staying seated when the world insists they stand aside.

Elizabeth did not change the law alone. But she forced it to respond to her presence.

That carriage ride did not just take her across the city. It helped redefine who the city was for.

4 Nancy Hart

Survival Becomes Legend

By the time history noticed Nancy Hart, she was already halfway to myth.

Stories about her are full of sharp edges. A tall woman. Wild hair. A temper to match the frontier she lived on. She carried a musket, spoke her mind, and was said to have no patience for British soldiers or anyone who supported them. Depending on who tells the story, she was fearless, ferocious, or downright dangerous.

What is harder to see, beneath the legend, is the woman who was simply trying to survive.

Nancy Hart lived on the western edge of the American colonies during the Revolutionary War, in a place where law was thin and violence was common. Frontier life offered little security, especially for women. Food was scarce. Raids were frequent. Allegiances could shift overnight. You learned quickly who could be trusted and who could not.

Nancy learned faster than most.

She was poor, unpolished, and outspoken. She did not fit the image of respectable womanhood even by frontier standards. That made her easy to dismiss and easy to underestimate. It also made her dangerous to cross.

The most famous story attached to her name involves a group of Loyalist soldiers who arrived at her cabin, demanding food and shelter. Nancy complied, at least at first. She fed them. She talked. She listened. She noticed their weapons stacked nearby.

When the moment came, she acted.

Accounts differ on the details, but the core remains the same. Nancy took control of the soldiers' guns and turned the tables. Some versions say she shot one of the men when he tried to overpower her. Others say her neighbors arrived in time to help capture them. What matters is not the precise sequence, but the reversal.

A woman alone in a cabin outwitted armed men who assumed she was harmless.

That story spread quickly. On the frontier, stories were currency. They warned enemies. They reassured allies. Nancy Hart became a name spoken carefully. British supporters learned to avoid her. Patriot forces treated her as a local asset.

Legend followed because it was useful.

Over time, Nancy's real life blurred into exaggeration. She was described as unnaturally strong, almost feral.

Her roughness became part of the appeal. She was no polished heroine. She was something closer to the land itself. Unpredictable. Unforgiving.

What often gets lost is why such stories took hold in the first place.

Nancy Hart did not have formal power. She did not command troops or hold office. She had her wits, her nerve, and an acute understanding of her environment. Survival required vigilance. It required the willingness to act before hesitation became fatal.

In a war where women were expected to endure quietly, Nancy refused to stay invisible. She used the assumptions made about her as cover. Her enemies mistook her for unimportant. She made that mistake costly.

After the war, her story softened. She was remembered as a colorful character rather than a strategic one. The danger she posed was rebranded as eccentricity. This is often what happens when women's violence is difficult to reconcile with accepted narratives. It becomes folklore instead of history.

But folklore preserves something history sometimes avoids. Emotional truth.

Nancy Hart's legend speaks to a reality of the Revolution that polished portraits rarely show. For many people, the war was not about ideology. It was about protecting homes, children, and food stores. It was about knowing when to smile and when to strike.

Survival, in that context, was not passive. It was active and sometimes brutal.

Nancy Hart did not set out to become a symbol. She responded to the world as it pressed in on her. The legend grew because people recognized something real in her story. A woman who refused to be overrun. A life shaped by necessity rather than permission.

History may never fully separate fact from embellishment in Nancy Hart's story. But the core remains credible and compelling. In places where safety was never guaranteed, survival itself was an act of defiance.

And sometimes, when survival leaves a strong enough impression, it becomes legend.

5 James Hemings

The Taste of Power
and the Price of Talent

James Hemings learned excellence in captivity.

He was born enslaved in Virginia and taken into the household of Thomas Jefferson as a child. From an early age, his intelligence and aptitude were noticed. In another life, that might have meant opportunity. In his, it meant investment. Jefferson recognized James's potential and decided to cultivate it, not for James's benefit, but for his own.

When Jefferson was appointed minister to France in the 1780s, he brought James Hemings with him. Paris was meant to refine Jefferson's tastes and status. James's role was to make that refinement edible.

In France, James was trained formally as a chef. He learned classical French techniques at a level few Americans could match at the time. He mastered sauces, pastries, and presentation. He absorbed a cuisine built on discipline, precision, and artistry.

He also learned something else. In France, slavery was illegal.

James could have stayed. The law would have protected him. He knew this. Jefferson knew it too. What followed was a quiet negotiation shaped by power. James agreed to return to America on one condition. He would be freed after training a replacement.

It was a bargain that reveals the cost of talent under slavery. James's freedom depended on teaching someone else to take his place. His skills were valuable, but only insofar as they could be transferred and retained by the household that owned him.

When Jefferson returned to the United States, James transformed American dining. He introduced dishes that are now considered staples. French fries. Ice cream prepared in the French style. Whipped desserts. Creamy sauces. Refined table service. The elegance associated with Jefferson's hospitality rested on James's hands.

Guests praised the meals. Jefferson's reputation grew. James remained enslaved.

Eventually, Jefferson honored the agreement. James Hemings was freed. He was one of very few people Jefferson ever manumitted.

Freedom did not resolve the imbalance that had shaped James's life.

He worked as a chef for wages, but his reputation was inseparable from the man who had owned him. He struggled financially. He moved often. He battled depression. The world admired the cuisine he helped introduce, but had little space for the person behind it.

James died young. He was thirty-six.

What makes his story difficult is not just the injustice, but the intimacy of it. James lived close to power. He served it daily. He elevated it. His talent made others appear sophisticated, worldly, and cultured. He received neither the security nor the recognition that usually follow such skill.

Food is often treated as background. Something enjoyed and forgotten. James Hemings's life reminds us that taste is never neutral. It is shaped by labor, by access, by whose hands are allowed to create and whose names are allowed to be remembered.

When Americans celebrate early national refinement, they rarely picture an enslaved man standing over a stove, translating European techniques into a new cultural language. They rarely ask who paid the price for that elegance.

James Hemings did not leave behind a cookbook. He left behind habits. Expectations. Standards. His influence survives every time American cuisine is described as inventive, hybrid, or refined.

His life forces an uncomfortable truth. Talent does not protect against exploitation. Proximity to power does not guarantee dignity. And brilliance, when owned by someone else, can be both a gift and a trap.

James Hemings shaped how a nation tasted itself. He did so at a cost history is still learning how to acknowledge.

6 Anton Wilhelm Amo

A Mind That Refused
to Be an Exception

Anton Wilhelm Amo did not want to be remarkable in the way people expected him to be.

He arrived in Europe as a child, taken from what is now Ghana and brought to Germany. He was presented as a curiosity at court, a symbol of exoticism rather than a person with a future. For many in his position, that might have been the end of the story. A life defined by display and dependence.

Amo chose something else.

He was educated seriously, not as a novelty but as a scholar. He studied philosophy, law, and medicine. He read the thinkers shaping European intellectual life and engaged them on their own terms. By the 1730s, Anton Wilhelm Amo was earning degrees and writing dissertations in Latin at major German universities.

This alone would have made him unusual. What made

him unsettling was how little he conformed to the role people wanted him to play.

Amo did not write about race as spectacle. He did not frame himself as an exception granted permission to think. He wrote about the mind, the body, and the limits of human knowledge. One of his most important works argued against the idea that the mind could feel physical pain, a philosophical intervention that placed him squarely inside contemporary debates rather than at their margins.

He was not asking to be included. He assumed he already was.

That assumption mattered. Europe in the eighteenth century was deeply invested in hierarchies. The presence of a Black philosopher teaching and publishing alongside white peers disrupted more than social norms. It challenged intellectual ones. Amo's work made it harder to argue that reason itself belonged to only one kind of person.

For a time, he succeeded on his own terms. He lectured. He published. He moved through academic circles with authority. Students listened to him. Colleagues engaged with his ideas.

But visibility has a cost.

As racial thinking hardened across Europe, Amo's position became more precarious. The novelty that had once opened doors began to close them. Subtle hostility replaced curiosity. Support faded. The institutions that had benefited from his presence no longer protected him.

Eventually, Amo left Europe and returned to Africa. Records of his later life are sparse. He appears to have lived quietly, far from the universities where he had once taught.

It is tempting to read this as a failure or a retreat. It is more accurate to see it as refusal.

Amo never performed gratitude for being allowed to participate. He never reshaped his work to make others comfortable. He did not accept the role of symbolic exception. He insisted on being measured by the same standards as everyone else, and when that became impossible, he withdrew rather than distort himself.

His legacy is subtle but profound. He stands as proof that the European Enlightenment was never as homogeneous as it later pretended to be. Black intellectual presence was not an anomaly. It was erased.

What makes Anton Wilhelm Amo easy to forget is that his life does not end in triumph or tragedy. It ends in quiet. No dramatic downfall. No public vindication. Just a mind that did its work and refused to apologize for existing.

In a world eager to celebrate rare exceptions, Amo offered something more radical. Normality. He claimed the right to think, teach, and argue without representing anything beyond his own ideas.

That insistence remains relevant. Progress is often framed as inclusion granted by institutions. Amo's life reminds us that true equality begins elsewhere. With the refusal to accept lesser terms. With the decision to belong without asking permission.

Anton Wilhelm Amo did not seek to be remembered as remarkable. He sought to be taken seriously.

History forgot him anyway.

7 Thayendanegea (Joseph Brant)

Negotiating a Future Already in Motion

Thayendanegea understood something early that many others refused to accept.

The world was changing whether he agreed to it or not.

Born into the Mohawk Nation in the eighteenth century, he grew up at a crossroads of languages, loyalties, and expectations. Europeans called him Joseph Brant, a name that made him legible to their records and politics. His Mohawk name tied him to land, kinship, and responsibility. He carried both, never fully able to set either down.

Brant was educated in English schools and moved comfortably in colonial society. He translated religious texts, spoke eloquently, and understood how power operated among the British. At the same time, he was deeply rooted in Haudenosaunee political traditions, where leadership meant persuasion rather than command.

This dual fluency made him valuable. It also made him suspect.

As tensions grew between Britain and the American colonies, Native nations were forced into impossible positions. Neutrality was rarely respected. Land was always the prize. Brant chose to ally with the British, believing they were more likely to honor treaties and restrain colonial expansion. It was not a romantic decision. It was a strategic one made under pressure.

War followed. Violence followed. Brant became a visible figure in a conflict that would later be remembered as a fight for liberty, even as it stripped Indigenous nations of land and autonomy. He was praised by some as a leader and condemned by others as a villain, often depending on who was writing the story.

After the war, the British lost. The Americans won. Indigenous nations paid.

Treaties were broken almost as soon as they were signed. Promises dissolved. Lands were claimed. Brant spent years traveling, negotiating, arguing, and pleading with colonial governments to honor agreements they had already made. He was not asking for dominance. He was asking for survival with dignity.

What makes Brant's life difficult to categorize is that he was not resisting a single force. He was navigating a collapsing system. The balance of power he had tried to manage was gone, replaced by a new nation eager to expand westward with little regard for those already there.

He secured land for his people in Canada. He fought legal battles. He wrote letters that reveal exhaustion as much as determination. Each negotiation came with diminishing returns.

History often prefers clear moral arcs. Heroes and villains. Winners and losers. Thayendanegea does not fit neatly into any of these. He made choices that saved lives and choices that haunted him. He worked within imperial systems while trying to protect a future that empire did not prioritize.

What remains remarkable is his realism.

Brant did not believe in going back. He believed in negotiating forward. Even when the future was already being shaped by forces far larger than him, he insisted on a seat at the table. He refused silence. He refused disappearance.

His story is not one of triumph. It is one of endurance under negotiation. Of leadership exercised in narrowing spaces. Of trying to secure continuity when collapse seems inevitable.

Thayendanegea knew that survival would not come from purity or isolation. It would come from adaptation, argument, and relentless presence. He spent his life insisting that his people were not relics of the past, but participants in the present.

The tragedy is not that he failed to stop change. No one could have. The tragedy is that his efforts are often remembered only through the wars he fought, not the futures he tried to protect.

He negotiated a future already in motion.

And in doing so, he left behind a record of leadership defined not by certainty, but by responsibility.

Part 2
Building Change from the Inside

From survival to agency, reform, and collective action. Day 8-14

8 Lemuel Haynes

Ideas That Traveled
Further Than Their Author

Lemuel Haynes began his life in silence.

He was born in 1753 to a white mother who abandoned him as an infant. A Black man took him in for a short time, then he was passed between households until he was eventually indentured to a white family in rural Massachusetts. There was no clear place for him in the world he entered. He belonged nowhere and to no one.

Books became his refuge.

The family he lived with owned few of them, but Haynes read everything he could find. He taught himself Latin, theology, and philosophy. He studied the Bible closely, not as a set of comforting verses, but as a moral argument. From an early age, he learned to listen for contradictions. Who was included in the promises of liberty and who was quietly excluded.

When the American Revolution began, Haynes joined the fight, serving in the militia. He believed, at least initially, in the language of freedom being used to justify it. But even as the war unfolded, he saw the gap between words and reality. The same leaders demanding independence continued to accept slavery as necessary.

Haynes responded the way he would for the rest of his life. He wrote.

In 1776, while the Revolution was still underway, Haynes penned an essay that did something radical. He applied the arguments being made for independence directly to the institution of slavery. If liberty was a natural right, he asked, how could it belong to some and not others? If tyranny was immoral, how could it be practiced by those who claimed to oppose it?

His words circulated quietly. They were read by clergy, by abolitionists, by people who recognized the force of the logic even if they were not ready to act on it.

Haynes did not stop there. He became a minister, one of the first Black men ordained in America. He preached to mostly white congregations for decades. This alone was extraordinary. What made it enduring was how he used the pulpit. He did not soften his message to preserve comfort. He insisted that faith without justice was hollow.

He wrote sermons and essays that argued against slavery, racial hierarchy, and moral hypocrisy. He framed equality not as a political concession, but as a spiritual obligation. His language was measured, reasoned, and difficult to dismiss. He did not shout. He reasoned.

Over time, his ideas traveled far beyond him. They were quoted. Referenced. Absorbed into broader abolitionist thought. Yet his name rarely followed them. White reformers echoed his arguments without always acknowledging their source. This was not unusual. It was how influence often moved.

Haynes himself lived modestly. He married. He raised children. He served small communities faithfully for years at a time. He did not seek national prominence. His power came from consistency rather than charisma.

What makes Lemuel Haynes easy to overlook is that he worked within existing structures. Church. Community. Print. He did not tear systems down. He pressed on their weak points until they bent.

His life reminds us that change does not always begin at the margins with spectacle. Sometimes it starts inside institutions, carried forward by people who understand their language well enough to expose their failures.

Lemuel Haynes did not live to see slavery abolished. He lived long enough to know his arguments would outlast him.

His ideas traveled further than he ever did. They moved through pulpits, pamphlets, and conversations he would never hear. Quietly, they helped prepare the ground for a reckoning still to come.

History often remembers the moment change becomes visible. It forgets the long work that made that moment possible.

Haynes did the long work.

9 James Forten
Building Power Without Permission

James Forten understood money as leverage.

He was born free in Philadelphia in 1766, a rare status that offered possibility but no guarantees. From an early age, he learned that freedom without power was fragile. Laws could shift. Mobs could form. Respect could disappear overnight. Security had to be built.

As a teenager, Forten went to sea, working aboard a privateer during the American Revolution. He was captured by the British and imprisoned on a prison ship. Offered his freedom in exchange for renouncing the American cause, he refused. Even then, he understood what allegiance meant and what it cost.

When he returned to Philadelphia, Forten found work in a sail loft. He learned the trade carefully, studying not just how sails were made, but how the business operated. When the owner died, Forten did something few Black men could do at the time. He bought the company.

Owning a business was not simply about income. It was about independence. As a successful sailmaker, Forten supplied ships that moved goods and people across the Atlantic. His work powered commerce. It also funded something else. Resistance.

Forten used his wealth to support abolitionist causes openly. He financed antislavery newspapers. He backed legal challenges. He offered assistance to formerly enslaved people trying to establish new lives. His home became a meeting place for activists, Black and white, who were pushing against a system designed to exclude them.

He was unapologetic about it.

At a time when many free Black Americans were encouraged to accept colonization plans that would remove them from the country, Forten spoke out forcefully against the idea. He insisted that Black Americans belonged where they were born. Citizenship, he argued, was not conditional.

His influence extended beyond money. Forten wrote essays and letters that circulated widely, challenging both slavery and the quieter racism of the North. He did not ask for gradualism. He demanded recognition.

What makes Forten's story distinctive is how deliberately he built power within the system he opposed. He did not wait for permission to participate in economic life. He entered it, mastered it, and used it to shape the political conversation.

He understood that moral arguments alone were rarely enough. Resources mattered. Infrastructure mattered. The ability to sustain movements over time mattered.

Forten raised a family that continued his work. His daughters became outspoken activists. His wealth became generational support for Black resistance in Philadelphia. Influence, for Forten, was something to be passed on.

He lived long enough to see abolitionist ideas gain traction, though not long enough to see slavery abolished. Still, his impact was tangible. Organizations existed because he funded them. Arguments survived because he paid to print them.

James Forten did not storm barricades or lead marches. He built something quieter and more enduring. A base.

In a society that told him to wait his turn, he refused. He built power without permission, and then he used it to widen the space for everyone who came after him.

10 Esther de Berdt Reed
When Domestic Work
Became Political

Esther de Berdt Reed understood the power of what women were already doing.

She lived in Philadelphia during the American Revolution, a city thick with arguments about liberty and independence. Men debated politics in taverns and assemblies. Women were expected to support the cause quietly, through sacrifice rather than strategy. Esther saw no reason to accept that division.

She was well connected, educated, and deeply aware of how households functioned during wartime. She knew who controlled supplies, who managed budgets, and who kept families and communities functioning while men were away fighting. That labor was constant and largely invisible.

Esther decided to make it visible.

In 1780, she helped organize a fundraising campaign aimed at women across the colonies. The idea was simple and radical. Women would contribute money directly to support soldiers, not as an act of charity directed by men, but as a political statement in their own right.

She wrote an address titled *The Sentiments of an American Woman*. In it, she argued that women had a stake in the outcome of the war and the right to act collectively. Patriotism, she suggested, was not confined to the battlefield.

The response was immediate. Women donated coins, jewelry, and savings. What might have seemed like small, domestic contributions accumulated into a significant fund. The effort spread beyond Philadelphia, reaching other states and inspiring similar initiatives.

Reed's project did more than raise money. It reframed women's work as political labor. Cooking, sewing, budgeting, and organizing were no longer just supportive tasks. They became acts of participation in the nation's future.

Esther did not live to see how far the idea would travel. She died suddenly in 1780, before the campaign reached its full impact. Others continued the work she had begun, distributing funds and expanding the network she envisioned.

History often credits wars to generals and politicians. It rarely accounts for the structures that made those efforts sustainable. Reed understood that revolutions are not won on ideals alone. They are sustained by logistics, coordination, and care.

Her insight feels strikingly modern. Social movements still rely on unpaid or underpaid labor, often performed by women, often dismissed as secondary. Reed's contribution was to insist that such labor mattered and that those who performed it deserved recognition as political actors.

She did not demand new roles for women. She elevated the ones they already occupied.

Esther de Berdt Reed did not march at the front of the Revolution. She organized behind the scenes, turning the rhythms of daily life into tools of resistance. In doing so, she helped expand the definition of political participation in ways that outlasted the war itself.

Domestic work did not stop being domestic.

It became political.

11 Hannah Griffitts

Poetry as a Record of Resistance

Hannah Griffitts did not think of herself as a revolutionary voice.

She lived in Philadelphia during the years leading up to and through the American Revolution, moving through a world shaped by Quaker values, community ties, and everyday responsibilities. She wrote poetry not for fame or publication, but because writing was how she paid attention.

That attention turned out to matter.

As tensions with Britain grew, Griffitts began to document what she saw around her. Shortages. Anger. Moral confusion. The unease of living through a moment when loyalty was constantly questioned and the future felt unstable. Her poems circulated quietly among friends and neighbors, copied by hand and passed along without ceremony.

They were not grand declarations. They were observations.

Griffitts wrote about spinning bees and boycotts, about women refusing imported goods, about the strain placed on households by political decisions made elsewhere. She captured the emotional texture of resistance. The fatigue. The stubborn resolve. The way ordinary life became politicized without anyone asking for it.

What makes her work distinctive is its grounding. She did not write from battlefields or legislative halls. She wrote from kitchens, streets, and meeting houses. Her poems remind us that political change is lived before it is declared.

Unlike many revolutionary writers, Griffitts did not frame the conflict as simple or glorious. She acknowledged fear and doubt alongside commitment. Her verses suggest a community negotiating its conscience in real time, unsure how far resistance should go and what it might cost.

Because she was a woman, and because her work circulated informally, Griffitts was never positioned as an official chronicler of the Revolution. Her poems were not preserved with the same care as speeches or pamphlets. Many survived only because someone thought they were worth copying.

That survival is meaningful.

Poetry often endures not because it is sanctioned, but because it resonates. Griffitts's writing mattered to the people who read it because it reflected their lives back to them. It named experiences that were otherwise swallowed by larger narratives of patriotism and progress.

She continued writing as the war unfolded, recording disappointment as well as hope. When the realities of independence failed to match its promises, her tone sharpened. She was not interested in mythology. She was interested in truth as it felt on the ground.

Hannah Griffitts did not change the course of the Revolution. She changed how it was remembered, at least for those who paid attention to the small details. Her poems preserve the inner life of resistance. The waiting. The worry. The quiet decisions that accumulate into change.

History often privileges declarations and outcomes. Griffitts offers something else. A record of how resistance was experienced day by day, by people who never expected to be remembered.

Her work reminds us that not all acts of resistance are loud. Some are written down carefully, shared quietly, and trusted to find their way forward.

Poetry, in her hands, became evidence.

12 Eliza Harriot O'Connor
Teaching Girls to Expect More

Eliza Harriot O'Connor believed expectations could be taught.

In the early nineteenth century, education for girls was often framed as a finishing exercise. Reading enough to follow scripture. Writing enough to manage household affairs. Knowledge was meant to decorate character, not expand it. O'Connor saw how limiting that vision was, and she refused to accept it.

She worked as a teacher and lecturer at a time when women speaking publicly about education were treated as curiosities at best and threats at worst. Rather than arguing that women were naturally different, she argued something far more unsettling. Girls had been trained to expect less, and society had organized itself around that lowered expectation.

Her classrooms reflected that belief. O'Connor taught girls to think critically, to ask questions, and to imagine futures beyond marriage and domestic duty. She treated them as intellectual beings whose minds deserved the same seriousness afforded to boys. This approach was not radical in theory. In practice, it was quietly disruptive.

O'Connor also lectured publicly on the importance of women's education, addressing mixed audiences who were not always comfortable hearing a woman articulate such ideas. She did not frame her arguments as rebellion. She framed them as common sense. Educated women, she insisted, strengthened families, communities, and nations.

That framing mattered. By grounding her case in social stability rather than individual ambition, she made it harder to dismiss. She spoke the language of improvement and responsibility, even as she pushed for expanded opportunity.

Still, resistance followed her. Women who encouraged girls to think independently were accused of unsettling social order. Education, critics warned, would make women dissatisfied with their proper roles. O'Connor understood that dissatisfaction was precisely the point. A girl who knew what she was capable of would notice when her world offered less.

Her influence did not come from a single institution or landmark reform. It spread through students who carried her expectations into their own lives. Through classrooms shaped by her methods. Through conversations that shifted what felt possible.

History often celebrates movements when they become visible. O'Connor's work operated earlier and quieter. She addressed the conditions that made inequality feel normal. She challenged them not with confrontation, but with preparation.

Teaching girls to expect more was not about promising ease or success. It was about giving them the tools to recognize when they were being underestimated. That recognition could change how they moved through the world.

Eliza Harriot O'Connor did not leave behind a famous manifesto. She left behind a generation of women who had been taught to take their own minds seriously.

Sometimes change begins not with demands, but with expectation.

13 Trota of Salerno
Writing Medicine
Before Doctors Listened

Trota of Salerno practiced medicine in a world that did not expect women to do so.

In the twelfth century, Salerno was one of Europe's most important medical centers. Its school attracted students from across the Mediterranean, blending Greek, Arabic, and Latin medical traditions. Knowledge flowed through the city, but authority remained tightly held. Learned medicine belonged to men, especially when it was written down.

Trota worked anyway.

She treated patients directly, especially women whose ailments were often ignored or misunderstood by male physicians. She observed bodies carefully and listened closely to symptoms. Where others relied on inherited theory, she relied on experience. Over time, that experience became text.

Trota wrote practical medical works focused on women's health, including childbirth, menstruation, and gynecological illness. These were subjects male physicians often avoided or approached with superstition rather than care. Trota addressed them plainly. Her writing assumed that women's pain mattered and that it could be treated with intelligence rather than shame.

That assumption was radical.

Her texts circulated widely and were copied for generations. They were used in medical training across Europe. For a time, her authority was accepted because her usefulness was undeniable. Patients improved. Midwives learned. Physicians borrowed.

Then something familiar happened.

As medical institutions became more formalized, Trota's identity became inconvenient. Scholars began to question whether a woman could have written such authoritative works. Her name was altered, merged, or erased. Over time, her writings were attributed to anonymous male authors or folded into collections known as the Trotula, treated as tradition rather than testimony.

Trota's knowledge survived. Her authorship did not.

This is not a story of exclusion through force. It is a story of exclusion through disbelief. The idea that a woman could produce lasting medical knowledge was easier to remove than the knowledge itself.

What makes Trota's work remarkable is how modern it feels. She emphasized observation over dogma. She valued patient experience. She treated women not as problems to be managed, but as people whose bodies required understanding on their own terms.

She did not write to challenge authority. She wrote to help.

Trota likely did not imagine her work would last centuries. She was addressing immediate needs. Pain. Illness. Survival. That practicality is precisely why her writing endured. It worked.

History tends to celebrate medicine when it becomes abstract or institutional. Trota reminds us that much of medical progress begins elsewhere. With someone paying attention. With someone recording what they see. With someone insisting that care should be guided by evidence rather than assumption.

She wrote medicine before doctors were ready to listen to women as sources of knowledge. Her reward was anonymity. Her legacy was influence without credit.

Trota of Salerno did not need recognition to matter. But remembering her now restores something important. The understanding that expertise has always existed outside the boundaries that institutions later tried to enforce.

She wrote anyway. And the world used her work, whether it acknowledged her or not.

14 Jeanne Villepreux-Power

Learning from the Sea
Instead of Conquering It

Jeanne Villepreux-Power did not set out to challenge science.

She set out to understand what she was looking at.

She was born in France in the late eighteenth century and trained originally as a dressmaker. Her hands were skilled, precise, and patient. Those same qualities would later shape her scientific work, though no one could have predicted that path. Science at the time was dominated by men, institutions, and grand theories. Jeanne approached it from the shoreline.

After moving to Sicily with her husband, she became fascinated by the sea. Not the dramatic storms or naval power that captured attention, but the small creatures living just beneath the surface. Mollusks, octopuses, organisms most naturalists studied only after they were dead.

That bothered her.

Specimens pulled from the ocean and preserved told only part of the story. Jeanne wanted to see how sea creatures lived, moved, and adapted. So she built something new. She designed glass containers that allowed marine animals to survive and be observed over time.

These were among the earliest aquariums.

It sounds obvious now. At the time, it was quietly revolutionary. Jeanne was not trying to dominate nature or dissect it into submission. She was trying to watch it. To let it behave as itself.

Her observations led to important discoveries, including evidence that the paper nautilus did not steal its shell, as many believed, but created it. This corrected long-standing assumptions repeated by respected male naturalists. Jeanne published her findings carefully, with clarity and restraint.

For a while, she was taken seriously.

Then recognition drifted away. Her work was cited without her name. Others repeated her conclusions as if they were common knowledge. When her contributions were acknowledged, they were often framed as charming rather than rigorous. Curiosity instead of expertise.

The pattern was familiar. Her ideas were absorbed. Her presence faded.

Jeanne continued her work despite setbacks. She corresponded with scientists, refined her methods, and persisted in observation as a way of knowing. She did not adopt the language of conquest that shaped much of natural science at the time. She resisted the urge to impose meaning too quickly.

Her approach feels strikingly modern. Ecology, environmental science, and conservation all depend on the principle that understanding comes from sustained attention rather than control. Jeanne practiced this instinctively.

Late in life, much of her work was lost or destroyed, and she faded into obscurity. The sea she had studied so closely did not preserve her name.

But her method survived.

Every time marine life is studied in living systems rather than extracted and reduced, her influence echoes. Every time scientists prioritize observation over assumption, they follow a path she helped open.

Jeanne Villepreux-Power reminds us that knowledge does not always advance through force or dominance. Sometimes it advances through care. Through patience. Through the willingness to sit still and watch.

She did not conquer the sea.

She listened to it.

And in doing so, she changed how it could be understood.

Part 3

The Quiet Architecture of Everyday Life

Inventions, systems, and safety. Day 15- 21

15 Margaret E. Knight

The Machine That
Changed How We Shop

Margaret E. Knight noticed problems other people walked past.

She grew up in the mid-nineteenth century with little formal education and even less encouragement. What she did have was a habit of paying attention. As a teenager working in a cotton mill, she watched machines injure workers and wondered why no one tried to make them safer. She sketched a device that could stop looms automatically when something went wrong. It was practical. It worked. No one bothered to patent it.

That pattern would repeat.

Knight went on to invent dozens of devices across her lifetime, but one changed daily life in a way most people never question. In the 1860s, paper bags were flimsy envelopes that tore easily and could not stand on their own. Shopping was messier than it needed to be.

Knight designed a machine that folded and glued paper bags with flat bottoms, allowing them to stand upright. It seems minor until you imagine commerce without it. Groceries, hardware, books. The simple act of carrying purchases depends on that quiet innovation.

When Knight tried to patent her machine, a man claimed the idea as his own. He argued that a woman could not have designed such a complex mechanism. The claim was taken seriously.

Knight did not argue abstractly. She brought her notebooks. She showed her sketches, models, and calculations. In court, she demonstrated not only that the machine was hers, but that she understood it in detail. She won.

The victory mattered beyond the patent. It affirmed that technical intelligence did not belong to one gender. Still, recognition remained limited. Knight was often described as eccentric rather than brilliant. Her inventions were useful, not celebrated.

That usefulness is the point.

Margaret E. Knight did not invent to impress. She invented to fix things. She saw inefficiencies and dangers and addressed them methodically. Her work made factories safer, packaging sturdier, and commerce smoother.

Today, her machine's legacy is everywhere and nowhere. Paper bags are so ordinary they are invisible. The genius behind them is rarely acknowledged. Convenience, when it becomes routine, tends to erase its origins.

Knight lived simply and died with modest means. She did not accumulate wealth equal to her impact. What she left behind was infrastructure. The unnoticed architecture of everyday life.

Her story reminds us that progress is often engineered quietly. It arrives without ceremony and stays without credit. The tools that shape daily habits rarely carry names.

Margaret E. Knight changed how we shop by solving a small problem extremely well. The fact that we no longer think about that problem is proof that she succeeded.

16 Josephine Cochrane

Turning Frustration into
a Household Revolution

Josephine Cochrane was tired of her dishes being broken.

She lived a comfortable life in late nineteenth-century America, hosting dinners that displayed both social standing and domestic competence. Fine china was part of the performance.

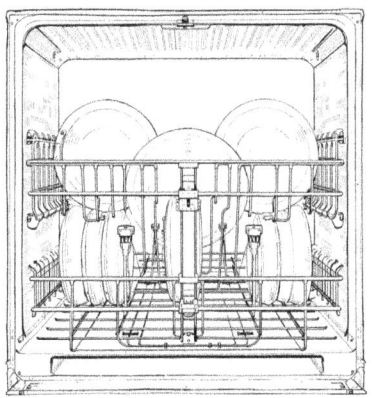

Servants washed the dishes by hand, and too often they chipped or cracked them. Josephine had a simple complaint that many people shared and few took seriously. There had to be a better way.

Most inventions begin with inconvenience. Hers began with irritation sharpened by necessity.

After her husband died, Josephine's financial security vanished. Hosting was no longer a hobby. It became a liability. She needed income, and she needed it without relying on skills society dismissed as unfeminine. So she turned to engineering.

Josephine did not wash dishes better. She redesigned the process entirely.

She measured plates and cups carefully, creating wire compartments that held them in place. She built a machine that sprayed hot water with controlled force, cleaning dishes efficiently without damage. Unlike earlier attempts, her design respected the objects it handled.

When she unveiled her dishwasher at the 1893 World's Columbian Exposition, the audience that paid attention was not the one she expected. Households were skeptical. Hotels and restaurants, however, immediately saw the value. Speed, consistency, and reduced breakage mattered to them.

Josephine adapted. She sold her machines to institutions first. Kitchens that needed reliability rather than novelty became her proving ground.

Her invention did not instantly liberate domestic labor as later advertising would claim. In many homes, dishwashers would not appear for decades. But the system she created laid the foundation for mechanized household work and changed expectations about cleanliness, time, and labor.

What often gets lost is how deliberate her work was. Josephine was not tinkering casually. She studied mechanics. She filed patents. She ran a manufacturing business. She navigated an industrial world that treated women as anomalies.

She rarely framed her success as a statement. She framed it as competence.

Josephine Cochrane's dishwasher worked because it respected the reality of the task. It acknowledged that repetitive labor deserved intelligent solutions. It treated domestic work as worthy of engineering, not just endurance.

Her revolution did not announce itself. It hummed quietly in kitchens that valued efficiency over spectacle. Over time, it reshaped how households imagined work, cleanliness, and time.

Josephine Cochrane turned frustration into infrastructure.

And once infrastructure is in place, life is never quite the same.

17 Nancy Johnson

Engineering Joy by Hand

Nancy Johnson did not set out to change dessert.

She wanted to make it easier.

In the early nineteenth century, ice cream was a luxury reserved for those with time, servants, and patience. Making it required constant stirring by hand, careful timing, and a willingness to endure cold for the sake of something fleeting. It was celebratory, but inconvenient.

Nancy noticed the imbalance.

In 1843, she patented a hand-cranked ice cream freezer that simplified the entire process. Her design used a rotating paddle inside a container surrounded by ice and salt. The motion froze the mixture evenly and efficiently. It was simple, durable, and accessible.

What she engineered was not indulgence. It was consistency.

For the first time, ordinary households could make ice cream without turning the kitchen into a test of endurance. Desserts became something to enjoy rather than manage. Pleasure, in this case, came from removing friction.

Nancy sold the patent for a modest sum. She did not build an empire or attach her name to a brand. Others profited far more from her idea than she did. Her invention spread quickly, becoming a standard fixture in homes and shops.

What makes her story easy to miss is its gentleness. There is no courtroom battle. No dramatic confrontation. Just a woman who identified a small joy and made it easier to reach.

That matters.

Not all progress is about survival or safety. Some of it is about delight. About making room for pleasure in ordinary life. Nancy Johnson understood that happiness, too, could be engineered.

Her ice cream maker did more than produce dessert. It changed social rituals. Ice cream socials became communal events. Celebrations became more inclusive. A treat once associated with privilege became part of shared culture.

Today, the device she designed has evolved, but its core principle remains. The rhythm of the hand crank. The patience rewarded. The sense that effort can be transformed into something sweet.

Nancy Johnson's legacy lives in the assumption that joy should be attainable, not extravagant. That comfort and celebration belong in everyday life.

She engineered joy by hand, then let it go.

And in doing so, she left behind something far more enduring than a patent. A habit of pleasure woven quietly into daily life.

18 Anne Connelly
Safety as a Radical Idea

Anne Connelly lived in a city that burned often.

Nineteenth-century New York was crowded, vertical, and dangerous. Buildings went up faster than safety standards could follow. Fires spread quickly through wooden structures packed with families, factories, and boardinghouses. When flames rose, escape was a matter of luck.

Anne paid attention to that luck, and she did not like its odds.

In 1887, she patented a fire escape designed to help people get out of buildings safely and quickly. It was practical, sturdy, and focused on one thing only. Survival. Not property. Not profit. People.

At the time, this focus was unusual.

Industrial progress celebrated speed, height, and output. Safety was often treated as an afterthought, especially for working-class residents whose lives were considered replaceable. Fires were framed as accidents rather than systemic failures.

Anne rejected that framing.

Her invention recognized a simple truth. People deserved a way out. Not after the fire started, not as an emergency improvisation, but as a built-in expectation. Escape should be part of the design, not a desperate hope.

We know little about Anne Connelly's life beyond the patent. That absence is telling. Safety innovators rarely become household names. When their work succeeds, disasters are avoided. When disasters are avoided, there is no spectacle to remember.

But her idea mattered.

Fire escapes became standard features of urban architecture. Over time, building codes changed. The expectation shifted from survival being accidental to safety being planned. Lives were saved quietly, repeatedly, without headlines.

Anne did not invent heroism. She invented foresight.

What makes safety radical is not the technology itself. It is the value system behind it. Choosing to prioritize human life over cost, convenience, or aesthetics requires imagining harm before it happens and caring enough to prevent it.

Anne Connelly's fire escape assumed that people would panic, that mistakes would happen, that emergencies were not moral failures. It treated vulnerability as a design requirement rather than a flaw.

That perspective still shapes how we live. Railings, exits, alarms, seatbelts. All of them exist because someone insisted that danger was predictable and therefore preventable.

Anne Connelly's contribution sits in the background of city life, barely noticed. That is its success.

Safety rarely announces itself. It waits, unused, until it is needed. And when it works, the story ends quietly, with people walking away.

She treated safety as a radical idea.

And then she made it ordinary.

19 Maria Beasley
Saving Lives Without Recognition

Maria Beasley believed preparation mattered more than praise.

She lived in the late nineteenth century, an era fascinated by progress and spectacle. Ships grew larger. Travel grew faster. Confidence outpaced caution. Safety was assumed rather than engineered, and disasters were treated as tragic exceptions instead of warnings.

Maria noticed the pattern.

She designed and patented an improved life raft, one that was collapsible, stable, and capable of being stored efficiently aboard ships. Her design addressed the realities of emergencies rather than ideal conditions. It assumed chaos, fear, and limited time.

That assumption saved lives.

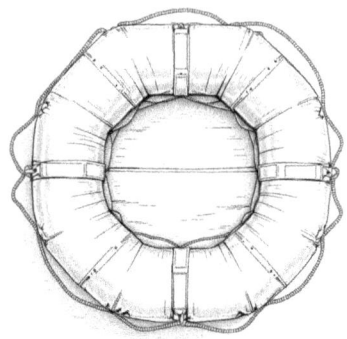

Her work was not limited to maritime safety. Maria also patented machines related to barrel making and industrial efficiency. She understood systems. How things moved. How they failed. How design choices shaped outcomes long before crises occurred.

Despite this, her name never became widely known. Safety does not advertise well. It becomes visible only when it is missing.

Maria's life rafts were adopted quietly. When disasters struck, survivors owed their lives not to heroics, but to design decisions made years earlier by someone they would never meet.

What makes Maria Beasley's story striking is how much responsibility she carried without recognition. She worked in a field that required technical skill, foresight, and persistence. She navigated patent systems that rarely took women seriously. She focused on function rather than acclaim.

Her inventions reflect a moral clarity that feels understated. People matter. Systems should reflect that.

In a world enamored with innovation that dazzles, Maria invested in innovation that protects. She did not chase the future. She prepared for its failures.

Her legacy is present in every safety device that prioritizes evacuation over elegance. In every system designed to hold steady under stress.

Maria Beasley saved lives without ever being named in the stories of survival. Her work reminds us that many of the people responsible for our safety remain invisible by design.

Recognition was never her product.

Reliability was.

And reliability, when it works, disappears into the background, carrying human lives with it.

20 Eleanor Coade

The Woman Who Built a
Material That Would Not Fade

The Woman Who Built a Material That Would Not Fade

Eleanor Coade made something that refused to crumble.

In eighteenth-century England, stone was a gamble. Statues cracked. Facades eroded. Weather and pollution took their toll quickly, especially in growing cities. Architecture aspired to permanence, but materials often failed the test.

Eleanor saw opportunity where others saw limitation.

She took over a struggling artificial stone business in London and transformed it. Through careful experimentation, she developed what became known as Coade stone, a ceramic-like material that could withstand time, frost, and urban air. It was strong, consistent, and adaptable.

It worked so well that people doubted it.

Many assumed a woman could not have been responsible for such a durable innovation. Eleanor allowed the material to speak for itself. She stamped her name on it, quite literally, embedding her identity into the product. This was not vanity. It was protection.

Architects and builders embraced Coade stone. It appeared on public buildings, bridges, monuments, and decorative sculptures. Unlike natural stone, it could be molded precisely and produced reliably. Unlike most materials of the era, it aged with dignity.

Eleanor ran the business herself. She managed production, marketing, and client relationships in a male-dominated industry. She insisted on quality control and refused shortcuts. Her reputation rested on consistency rather than novelty.

What makes her story unusual is not just the invention, but the endurance. Many innovations fade or are replaced. Coade stone remains visible today, centuries later, in architectural details that look remarkably intact.

Eleanor did not frame her work as revolutionary. She framed it as dependable. That dependability built trust and, over time, legacy.

History often celebrates creators whose work is dramatic or fragile. Eleanor Coade's contribution was the opposite. It was resilient. It stayed.

She built a material that carried her name forward even as her personal story receded. Visitors admire the craftsmanship without knowing who made it possible.

Eleanor Coade understood that permanence is power. By creating something that would not fade, she ensured that her influence would outlast trends, reputations, and even memory.

Her work still stands.

That is her signature.

21 Henrietta Vansittart

Making the World Move Faster

Henrietta Vansittart learned engineering the way many women of her era did. By necessity, observation, and persistence.

She grew up around invention. Her father was an engineer and inventor who spent years experimenting with ship propulsion, convinced that traditional propellers were inefficient and poorly suited to large vessels. Henrietta watched closely. She learned the mechanics not from textbooks or formal training, but from workshops, sketches, and unfinished ideas spread across a working life.

When her father died, his work was incomplete and largely dismissed.

Henrietta refused to let it disappear.

She took his designs seriously enough to improve them. She refined a propeller shape that reduced vibration, increased speed, and improved fuel efficiency. These were not cosmetic adjustments. They addressed real problems faced by an expanding industrial world dependent on maritime transport.

She patented the improved propeller under her own name.

That decision alone was an act of quiet defiance. Engineering patents were overwhelmingly male territory. Women were expected to support innovation, not claim it. Henrietta did not argue for permission. She demonstrated results.

Her propellers were tested on ships and proved effective. They moved faster and more smoothly. For a time, her work gained recognition. She was awarded a prize at an international exhibition and consulted on naval engineering projects.

Then attention shifted elsewhere.

Technological progress is crowded. New ideas compete not only on merit, but on networks, capital, and credibility. Henrietta's contributions were absorbed into a broader field that rarely credited women as originators. Her name faded even as her ideas continued to shape propulsion systems.

What makes her story compelling is how directly it connects to modern life. Faster ships meant quicker trade, communication, and travel. They altered economies and expectations. Henrietta's work helped compress distance in a world growing rapidly more connected.

She did not invent speed. She optimized it.

Henrietta Vansittart understood that progress is not only about breakthroughs. It is about refinement. About noticing inefficiencies and refusing to accept them as inevitable. Her improvements made the machinery of modern life move more smoothly, even if few paused to ask who was responsible.

She did not become a household name. But the world she helped accelerate never slowed back down.

Henrietta Vansittart made the world move faster by solving problems others overlooked. Her legacy travels quietly beneath the surface, carried forward by every system that values precision over spectacle.

Part 4
Expanding the World

Travel, taste, science, and ideas. Day 22- 28

22 Sake Dean Mahomed

Reinventing the Self Across Empires

Sake Dean Mahomed understood that identity could be negotiated.

He was born in India in the mid-eighteenth century and grew up within the structures of empire. As a young man, he served in the East India Company's army, moving through a world shaped by hierarchy and displacement. When he left India for Europe, he carried more than memories. He carried the question of who he would be allowed to become.

Mahomed arrived in Ireland first, then later in England. He did not try to disappear into the background. He introduced himself deliberately, shaping a public identity that combined familiarity and difference. He learned how to speak to British audiences without flattening himself entirely.

In 1794, he published a book describing his experiences in India. It was the first known book in English by an

Indian author. Rather than exoticizing his homeland, Mahomed wrote with intimacy and specificity. He assumed readers were capable of understanding complexity.

That assumption was ambitious.

Mahomed continued reinventing himself. He married an Irish woman, opened one of Britain's first Indian restaurants, and later became known for popularizing "shampooing," a form of therapeutic massage and bathing inspired by South Asian practices. His bathhouse attracted elite clients, including royalty.

Each reinvention was strategic.

Mahomed did not passively absorb imperial culture. He adapted it. He translated his knowledge into forms that could survive and thrive within British society. Food became a bridge. Touch became expertise. Storytelling became authority.

What makes his life remarkable is its range. Soldier. Author. Restaurateur. Entrepreneur. Each role built on the last, creating continuity where empire usually imposed fracture.

Mahomed's success did not mean acceptance without limits. He remained visible as different. His achievements were framed as novelty as often as accomplishment. Yet he persisted, reshaping how Britain experienced Indian culture long before multiculturalism had a name.

His influence is still present. British tastes, wellness practices, and literary history carry traces of his work. They rarely credit him directly.

Sake Dean Mahomed did not conquer empire. He navigated it. He treated identity as something flexible enough to survive displacement without disappearing.

He reinvented himself across empires not to escape who he was, but to make space for it.

And in doing so, he expanded what belonging could look like.

23 Jeanne Baret
Around the World in Disguise

Jeanne Baret wanted to see the world.

The world did not want to see her.

In the eighteenth century, women were barred from naval expeditions. Exploration was framed as masculine by definition, a test of endurance and authority. Jeanne understood the rule clearly enough to break it.

She disguised herself as a man and boarded a French ship bound for a global voyage of exploration. Her role was official, even if her identity was not. She served as assistant to a naturalist, managing specimens, organizing collections, and doing the physical labor required to document the natural world.

The work was demanding and unglamorous. Plants had to be collected, preserved, and cataloged in difficult conditions. Heat, illness, and exhaustion were constant. Jeanne did not falter.

For years, she maintained her disguise. Crew members noticed differences but hesitated to name them. The ship moved from continent to continent. The world expanded beneath her feet.

Eventually, her identity was discovered. The consequences were serious. She was exposed to ridicule, danger, and isolation. Yet by then, she had already accomplished something unprecedented.

Jeanne Baret became the first woman to circumnavigate the globe.

Her contributions to botany were substantial. She collected and prepared thousands of plant specimens, many of which were new to European science. Some were later named after the man she worked for. Her labor was essential, her credit partial.

Disguise was her entry point. Competence was her justification.

Jeanne's story is often told as a curiosity, a tale of audacity and deception. What deserves more attention is the cost. Living in disguise meant constant vigilance. One mistake could have ended her journey or her life. She carried not only equipment, but fear.

Yet she persisted because the work mattered.

Jeanne Baret did not travel for fame or conquest. She traveled to participate in knowledge-making. She wanted to touch the world and record it accurately. That desire outweighed the risk.

Her voyage expanded scientific understanding while challenging the boundaries placed around women's bodies and ambitions. She proved that exploration was not about gender, but about endurance, skill, and resolve.

Jeanne did not return home celebrated. She returned changed.

History often remembers explorers as figures who imposed themselves on the world. Jeanne Baret reminds us that exploration can also be an act of access. Of insisting on participation in a realm that has been declared off-limits.

She went around the world in disguise not to hide who she was, but to reach where she was not allowed to go.

And once there, she did the work.

24 Lewis Latimer
Drawing the Future by Hand

Lewis Latimer understood that ideas only matter if they can be built.

He was born in 1848 to parents who had escaped enslavement, and his early life was shaped by instability and self-reliance. Formal education was limited. Opportunity was uncertain. What Latimer developed instead was skill. He taught himself mechanical drawing, mastering the ability to translate concepts into precise, usable plans.

That skill became his entry point.

Latimer was hired as a draftsman in a patent law office, where his drawings helped secure some of the era's most important inventions. He worked on the technical plans for Alexander Graham Bell's telephone, producing clear, detailed illustrations that allowed the idea to move from concept to protected innovation.

Later, Latimer joined the race to bring electric light into everyday life. He worked with and alongside major figures of the electrical age, improving the carbon filament that made light bulbs longer-lasting and more affordable. His refinements helped electricity move out of laboratories and into homes.

Latimer's contributions were technical, practical, and essential. They were also easily overlooked.

Invention culture celebrates visionaries. It rarely celebrates the people who make visions functional. Latimer was one of those people. He solved problems others did not want to see. Durability. Cost. Scalability.

He also navigated a professional world that did not expect Black men to occupy technical authority. Latimer responded with excellence rather than confrontation. His competence made him indispensable, even if it did not guarantee recognition.

He wrote one of the first technical manuals on electric lighting, helping train engineers and installers as the technology spread. Knowledge, for Latimer, was something to be shared, not guarded.

What makes his story powerful is its quietness. There is no single breakthrough moment. There is sustained contribution. Drawing after drawing. Improvement after improvement.

Latimer understood that progress depends on translation. Someone must take an idea and make it legible to others. He did that work with care and precision.

The future he helped shape was bright, literal and figurative. Streets lit at night. Homes illuminated. Work extended beyond daylight.

Lewis Latimer drew that future by hand.

Line by line, he made innovation usable.

History often credits those who dream. Latimer reminds us that the world also belongs to those who know how to make dreams work.

25 Eunice Newton Foote

Discovering the Warming World Too Soon

Eunice Newton Foote asked a simple question and arrived at an uncomfortable answer.

In the mid-nineteenth century, science was becoming more formal, more institutional, and more closed to women. Eunice worked outside those institutions. She was curious, methodical, and willing to test ideas herself rather than wait for permission.

She experimented with glass cylinders, thermometers, and different gases. She wanted to know how heat behaved. What she discovered was quietly astonishing. Air containing carbon dioxide heated up more and retained heat longer than ordinary air.

She understood the implication.

If the atmosphere contained more of this gas, she reasoned, the planet itself would warm. Climate, she suggested, was not fixed. It could change.

In 1856, Eunice presented her findings at a scientific meeting. She did not read the paper herself. Women were not allowed to speak. A man delivered her work on her behalf.

The room listened. The idea registered. And then it drifted away.

Her discovery did not fit neatly into the priorities of the time. Industrial growth was accelerating. Coal powered progress. Few wanted to consider the possibility that human activity could alter the planet's balance.

Later, similar conclusions were credited to male scientists whose names became attached to climate science. Eunice's contribution was sidelined, not because it was wrong, but because she was early and inconvenient.

That combination is often fatal to recognition.

What makes her story especially striking is how clearly she saw the connection between atmosphere and temperature using modest tools. No satellites. No supercomputers. Just careful observation and logic.

She did not frame her work as a warning. She presented it as evidence. The warning only became clear in hindsight.

Eunice Newton Foote discovered a warming world before the world was ready to listen. Her insight sat quietly in the record while the conditions she described slowly took shape.

Today, her work reads as prophetic. Not because she predicted catastrophe, but because she recognized cause and effect long before it became undeniable.

She reminds us that science does not always fail because it lacks data. Sometimes it fails because it arrives too early, carried by someone society is not prepared to hear.

Eunice saw the future warming.

The tragedy is not that she was wrong.

It is that she was right.

26 Sophie Germain

Thinking in Secret to
Be Taken Seriously

Sophie Germain learned early that knowledge could be dangerous.

Born in eighteenth-century France, she grew up in a household where intellectual curiosity was discouraged, especially for girls. When the French Revolution erupted, Sophie found refuge in books. Mathematics became her sanctuary, pursued late at night by candlelight after her family tried to lock it away.

They worried it would harm her.

She worried she would lose it.

Formal education was closed to her, so Sophie created her own. She studied advanced mathematics in isolation, teaching herself subjects that universities reserved for men. When she began corresponding with leading mathematicians, she used a male pseudonym to ensure her work would be read rather than dismissed.

It worked.

Her ideas were taken seriously. Her proofs were debated. Only later did some of her correspondents realize they had been engaging with a woman. Reactions ranged from surprise to discomfort. Respect did not always survive the revelation.

Sophie persisted anyway.

She made significant contributions to number theory and mathematical physics, including work that laid groundwork for understanding elasticity and vibration. Her research helped explain how structures respond to stress, knowledge that later influenced engineering and architecture.

Recognition came slowly and incompletely. She won a prestigious prize for her work, yet was never fully welcomed into the academic world she had helped advance. She was celebrated as an exception rather than accepted as a peer.

That framing cost her.

Sophie Germain spent much of her intellectual life working alone, not by preference, but by necessity. She thought in secret so her ideas could move freely. The concealment protected her work even as it erased her presence.

What makes her story resonate is not just her brilliance, but her endurance. She continued despite isolation, illness, and limited validation. She pursued truth for its own sake.

Sophie Germain did not ask to be admired. She asked to be understood.

Her life reveals how often brilliance has been filtered through disguise, patience, and persistence. How much knowledge exists because someone refused to stop thinking, even when recognition was withheld.

She thought in secret so the world could build in public.

And long after the secrecy faded, her ideas remained.

27 Oliver Heaviside

Changing the World
Without Leaving the Room

Oliver Heaviside did not belong to institutions, and he did not try to.

He left school at sixteen with little formal education and even less patience for authority. He was shy, increasingly reclusive, and deeply uninterested in social performance. What he had instead was an extraordinary ability to think clearly about difficult problems and a stubborn refusal to accept explanations that felt unnecessarily complicated.

He taught himself mathematics and physics at a time when both fields were becoming professionalized and exclusionary. He worked alone, often from small rented rooms, filling notebooks with ideas that few around him understood and even fewer were willing to champion.

Heaviside believed that clarity mattered more than tradition.

One of his most significant contributions was simplifying James Clerk Maxwell's complex equations governing electromagnetism. Maxwell's original work was brilliant but unwieldy. Heaviside rewrote it into a more usable form, making it practical for engineers and scientists. Modern electrical engineering rests on this simplification.

He also developed mathematical tools that allowed signals to be analyzed and transmitted more efficiently. His work made long-distance communication possible, from telegraphy to radio. He predicted the existence of an atmospheric layer that reflects radio waves back to Earth, enabling global communication. The idea was later confirmed and became known as the Heaviside layer.

These were not small insights. They reshaped how the world connected.

Yet Heaviside remained on the margins. He struggled financially. He fell out with colleagues. His personality made collaboration difficult, and institutions rarely reward people who do not conform to their rhythms. Recognition came late, partial, and often reluctantly.

He did not help himself by refusing to explain his ideas in socially acceptable ways. He valued precision over politeness. He dismissed what he saw as intellectual clutter without apology. This made him correct and isolated.

What makes Heaviside's life compelling is the scale of his impact compared to the smallness of his circumstances. He did not lead teams. He did not run laboratories. He rarely traveled. Much of his work was done alone, sitting at a desk, thinking.

And yet his ideas escaped the room he lived in.

They traveled through wires, signals, equations, and eventually the infrastructure of the modern world. Telephones. Radios. Electrical grids. The invisible systems that allow information to move depend on principles he clarified.

Oliver Heaviside reminds us that progress does not always look collaborative or well adjusted. Sometimes it looks like a solitary figure refusing to stop thinking.

He changed the world without leaving the room, not because he avoided society, but because he trusted ideas enough to follow them wherever they led.

History tends to celebrate visibility. Heaviside's legacy challenges that instinct. Influence does not require presence. It requires precision.

And precision, when it works, travels farther than any person ever could.

28 Jeanne Villepreux-Power
Listening Long Enough to Change the Scale

Jeanne Villepreux-Power ended where she began.

With attention.

By the end of her life, she had watched the sea more closely than most people ever would. Not as metaphor. Not as backdrop. As a living system, full of patterns that only revealed themselves to those willing to wait.

She never believed knowledge had to be loud to be real.

Jeanne's work did not produce a single dramatic discovery that could be pointed to as a turning point. What it produced instead was a method. Observation over extraction. Patience over dominance. Careful record over assumption. This approach quietly shifted how natural science could be practiced.

That shift matters more than it first appears.

Science often advances by narrowing focus, isolating variables, and controlling conditions. Jeanne expanded the frame. She allowed life to unfold in front of her. She built spaces where creatures could remain alive long enough to be understood. She accepted complexity rather than forcing conclusions.

This was not a refusal of rigor. It was a different kind of rigor.

By the time she faded from view, the world she helped shape was already moving beyond her. Marine biology was becoming formalized. Institutions took over. Credit reorganized itself around titles and affiliations she never had.

But her influence remained embedded.

Every field that studies ecosystems rather than specimens owes something to her instinct. Every scientific practice that values long-term observation over quick results echoes her approach. She helped scale knowledge outward, from isolated facts to living systems.

Ending this book with Jeanne Villepreux-Power is deliberate.

She represents what these twenty-eight lives share. Not fame. Not certainty. But impact achieved through sustained attention. Through staying with a problem longer than others were willing to. Through working without guarantees.

Jeanne did not conquer the sea. She did not map it or claim it. She respected it enough to learn from it. That respect allowed her ideas to outlast her recognition.

History often measures importance by volume. By how loudly a name is repeated. Jeanne reminds us that some of the most transformative work happens quietly, accumulating over time until it reshapes how we see the world.

She listened long enough for scale to emerge.

And in doing so, she leaves us with a final lesson. Change does not always announce itself. Sometimes it arrives slowly, through care, patience, and the refusal to look away.

That kind of attention can still change everything.

What These Lives Ask of Us

These lives do not ask for admiration.

They ask for attention.

None of the people in this book lived with the assurance that their work would be remembered. Most had no reason to believe it would be. They acted within the limits of their circumstances, often without recognition, often without protection, and sometimes without knowing whether their efforts would matter at all.

That uncertainty is the thread that binds them.

We tend to tell history as if impact is obvious in the moment. As if change announces itself clearly, wearing the right name and standing in the right place. These lives tell a different story. Change is often incremental. It happens inside systems rather than outside them. It is built quietly, piece by piece, by people who refuse to stop paying attention.

What these stories ask of us is not to turn them into heroes. Hero worship flattens complexity and distances us from responsibility. Instead, they invite us to reconsider how influence actually works.

Many of these people were not the loudest voices in the room. Some were not allowed in the room at all. They worked anyway. They wrote, taught, built, observed, negotiated, and refined. They did not wait for ideal conditions. They responded to the world as it was.

That matters now.

We live in a time that rewards visibility and speed. Success is often measured by scale and immediacy. These lives remind us that durability is another measure. That some of the most important work happens slowly, without applause, and without certainty of reward.

They also ask us to be more careful about what we inherit without question. The systems we rely on, the knowledge we accept, the comforts we assume. Each has a history shaped by labor that may not be named. Remembering that does not diminish progress. It deepens it.

Finally, these lives ask us to reconsider our own expectations. Not of greatness, but of contribution. Most change does not come from singular moments of courage. It comes from sustained commitment. From returning to a problem. From refusing to let something important slip out of view.

You do not need to change the world all at once.

Neither did they.

They paid attention. They acted within their reach. They accepted that recognition might not follow.

History forgot them for a time.

That forgetting was never proof they did not matter.

What remains is the question they leave us with.

What quiet work is being done now, and who will notice it later.

The answer depends, in part, on whether we learn to look.

Sources and Further Reading

This book was written with care for historical accuracy, but also with an understanding that many of the lives it explores survive in fragments. Court records, patents, letters, sermons, scientific papers, and contemporary accounts often tell us more about systems than about people. Wherever possible, primary sources were prioritized, alongside modern scholarship that reexamines overlooked figures with greater context and nuance.

Below is a starting point for readers who want to go deeper.

Primary Sources and Historical Records

- Court petitions, freedom suits, and colonial legal records from New Netherland and early New York

- Patent filings and technical drawings from the United States and Britain

- Sermons, essays, and correspondence circulated during the American Revolutionary period

- Proceedings and papers from nineteenth-century scientific societies

- Ship logs, expedition records, and botanical catalogs from eighteenth-century voyages

Many of these materials are held in national archives, university libraries, and digital public collections.

Biographical and Scholarly Works

- Academic histories of slavery, abolition, and early Black intellectual life in the Atlantic world

- Studies of women inventors, engineers, and scientists before formal inclusion in institutions

- Scholarship on Indigenous diplomacy and leadership during the colonial and early national periods

- Works on the history of medicine, domestic technology, and industrial design

- Research on early climate science, electromagnetism, and marine biology

Modern historians, archivists, and librarians have been essential in recovering these lives from obscurity.

Museums, Archives, and Public Collections

- National and regional archives in the United States, United Kingdom, France, Germany, and Italy

Sources and Further Reading

- Museum collections focused on science, industry, and social history
- University special collections and digitized manuscript libraries
- Historical societies preserving local records often overlooked by national narratives

Many of these institutions now make their holdings freely accessible online.

Recommended General Reading

- Books on microhistory and everyday life in historical periods
- Studies of how systems, technologies, and cultural practices evolve over time
- Works examining how historical memory is shaped, erased, and recovered

These broader perspectives help place individual lives within the worlds they navigated.

A Note on Historical Silence

Some gaps remain. In several cases, especially for women, enslaved people, and those excluded from formal power, the historical record is incomplete. Silence in the archive is itself part of the story. Where details are missing, this book has avoided speculation and focused instead on what can be responsibly known.

Sources and Further Reading

Remembering these lives does not close the record. It opens it.

Readers are encouraged to continue the work. To question what is missing. To look beyond the familiar names. And to treat history not as a finished account, but as an ongoing conversation shaped by who is willing to pay attention.

Acknowledgements

This book exists because of people who paid attention.

Archivists, librarians, historians, and researchers preserve lives that history would otherwise leave behind. Much of the work they do happens quietly, without recognition, and often under conditions that make long-term care difficult. Their commitment made this book possible.

I am grateful to the scholars who have spent years revisiting footnotes, questioning omissions, and refusing to accept inherited narratives at face value. Their work provided the foundation for these pages. Any clarity here is borrowed from their persistence.

Thanks are also due to the institutions that have opened their collections to the public. Access matters. Many of the stories in this book survive because documents were preserved and, just as importantly, made visible.

Acknowledgements

To editors, early readers, and careful critics who challenged tone, pacing, and assumptions, thank you. This book is stronger because of your insistence on precision and restraint.

I am especially indebted to writers, past and present, who believe that history can be told without spectacle and still carry weight. Their influence shaped not just how these lives are described, but why they are worth describing at all.

Finally, thank you to the reader.

You chose to spend time with lives that history did not center. That choice matters. Attention is not neutral. It is a form of respect.

If this book encourages you to look more closely at the systems you inhabit, the stories you inherit, or the quiet work happening around you, then it has done what it set out to do.

- **Edwin Hale**

www.ingramcontent.com/pod-product-compliance
Lightning Source LLC
Chambersburg PA
CBHW042044280426
43661CB00094B/1012